AXOLOTL

The ultimate guide book on how to care, feed, house, common health issues of axolotl

RICHARD MICHAEL

Table of Contents

CHAPTER ONE

INTRODUCTION

The axolotl might not be a completely not unusual puppy, however it's miles truly a completely unique one. Axolotls are a kind of salamander, however unlike salamanders, they do now not automatically go through metamorphosis from the larval (with gills) to adult shape and remain aquatic their complete lifestyles. Axolotls may be located in a variety of colors including black, gray, golden, albino, white with black eyes, and other shades.

They may be surprisingly smooth to take care of, but they stay their entire lives in water, so that you must be capable of offer an adequate tank this is saved on the right temperature for this animal.

Axolotls are exceptionally hardy animals. They may be tame in nature. Those creatures should be concept

Of as a show puppy on account that they cannot interact with their puppy owners out of doors of their tank. They are sensitive, soft-bodied amphibians with permeable pores and skin. Axolotls need to no longer be treated unless truly important. They are no longer especially social animals and do no longer gain from having an accomplice.

CHAPTER TWO

HOUSING YOUR AXOLOTL

Axolotls can get pretty big for a salamander, so at the least a 15 to 20 gallon fish tank (aquarium) is usually recommended, despite the fact that the tank does not should be full of water (the water only needs to be simply deeper than the whole duration of the axolotl).

The tank should be kept in a fab room away from shiny sunlight. The water temperature should be saved cool, between 57 and 68 levels Fahrenheit (14 and 20 stages Celsius), and in no way allowed to get above 75 F (24 C). No unique lighting is required for axolotls (not like reptiles), and actually, a place to get out of the light can be liked, such as a flower pot laid on its side or an aquarium castle.

If gravel is used on the bottom of the tank, it wishes to be coarse gravel. Great gravel might be ingested at some stage in feeding and motive an obstruction. A few proprietors opt to virtually depart the lowest of the tank bare, although others accept as true with this can stress the axolotls a chunk when you consider that they cannot get a foothold on the lowest of the tank without gravel.

Juvenile axolotls may be cannibalistic towards each other, so they're nice raised in separate enclosures. Adults can doubtlessly be housed together but watch for cannibalistic inclinations. If a body component gets bitten off via a tank mate, an axolotl can regenerate it over time, however this have to never be encouraged or allowed.

Maximum proprietors will find a filtered aquarium simpler to preserve than one without a filter out because unfiltered water will need common changing. However, if you do choose to have a clear out on the tank, the filtration price must be fairly slow, and powerful filters that create strong currents have to be averted. Also, be sure that the clear out consumption isn't in a function to entice the gills of your axolotl.

When you have a filter out, safe cleaning might include the usage of a siphon to vacuum the lowest of the tank, and a 20 percentage water trade have to be accomplished weekly. Maybe in case you are not the usage of a filter, you ought to do a 20 percentage water alternate every day or every other day. In no way do full water alternate as this creates a scenario wherein the water chemistry changes too drastically to your pet axolotl.

Faucet water have to have any chlorine or chloramines (brought at some stage in the water treatment process) removed the use of commercially to be had answers. Never use distilled water and make sure the pH of the water remains among 6.5 and 7.5 (neutral).

CHAPTER THREE
FEEDING YOUR AXOLOTL

In the wild, axolotls feed on snails, worms, crustaceans, small fish, and small amphibians. In captivity, they may be fed a diffusion of brine shrimp, small strips of pork or liver, earthworms (though wild stuck worms can convey parasites), bloodworms, tubifex worms (frequently fed to fish), other frozen fish meals, or industrial fish pellets which includes salmon or trout pellets. Pellets also can be purchased directly from the University of Kentucky wherein they breed and distribute axolotls to laboratories and lecture rooms thru their Ambystoma Genetic stock middle. Uneaten meals need to be cleaned from the tank daily to assist preserve the tank smooth.

CHAPTER FOUR

COMMON HEALTH PROBLEMS OF AXOLOTL

Beneath some circumstances, the axolotl can go through metamorphosis right into a terrestrial from, despite the fact that this will be annoying on the animal and isn't always usually seen. The conditions underneath which this will take place naturally is poorly understood, however we recognize that the metamorphosis may be induced the use of adjustments in water characteristics, or by way of supplementing the axolotl with certain proportions of thyroid hormone. Of direction, the terrestrial shape of the axolotl has a very different set of care requirements. Seeking to induce metamorphosis isn't endorsed, as this can place undue stress on an axolotl, and may drastically shorten its lifespan.

Axolotls often consume gravel or a part of their substrate and are normally prone to gastrointestinal obstruction and overseas frame ingestion. Bowel obstructions are a not unusual reason of death and gravel and other objects in the tank ought to be cautiously sized.

CHAPTER FIVE

TYPES OF WATER TO KEEP AXOLOTL

For the reason that axolotls absorb water and oxygen via their skin, the kind of water this is used in their homes may be very important to their fitness. Many human beings might not comprehend that there's a distinction among distilled, bottled, tap, and other varieties of water, but the differences are a massive deal and do rely.

It may not sound essential, but the kind of water you use to keep your puppy axolotl wet can play a sizable role in his basic fitness. Agree with it or now not, the forms of water you get from your faucet, refrigerator, bottles, jugs, and outdoor circulate are all unique, and a few are safer than others. Minerals and salts are essential for the water you select, at the same time as chemical compounds like fluoride and chlorine are not. A neutral pH of 7.0 is ideal, even as a pH under 6.5 and over 8.5 is unsafe.

Bottled Water

Axolotls, like salamanders and newts, want the minerals which can be determined in herbal water and include sodium chloride, potassium chloride, and others. Bottled water is commonly spring water this is treated but then has these herbal minerals and salts introduced in. Bottled water is the most secure sort of water to present on your amphibian, and you do not have to modify it in any manner. Examine the label of the bottled water to ensure it isn't really distilled water and that it's been dealt with by using reverse osmosis, filtration, or any other kind of system to eliminate chemical compounds.

Town faucet Water

Relying on what you live in and what metropolis, state, province, or district filtration practices arise, the contents of your tap water can range significantly from place to area. in case you use your faucet water for your puppy, then you definitely need to both allow the water take a seat for 24 hours to allow the chlorine expend or cast off the chlorine with unique de-chlorination drops (like DeChlor) you buy at the pet keep. A few cities now use chloramines in place of chlorine inside the water, which can be more difficult to take away. Take a look at your water invoice to look if it's far indexed or call the water department to see if the water is aquarium fish safe. In case you aren't certain, you're better off now not using tap water.

Well Water

In case you use well water as opposed to city water in your own home, you could or might not be capable of using it with your axolotl; however you'll have to check it to discover. A few well water is simply too high in iron or has an inappropriate pH for amphibians. Other times it is not properly oxygenated. The pH may be examined the use of check strips in the aquarium segment on the pet store to make certain the water is set 7.0 or impartial, and the oxygenation and iron issues can be resolved with the aid of aerating the water. This will be done with the usage of a simple aerator offered in the fish department.

Distilled Water

You ought to in no way use distilled water with your puppy. Distilled water has none of the critical minerals and salts that amphibians require from their water, has greater hydrogen than tap water or bottled water, and has an acidic pH (less than 7.0). All of these versions make distilled water risky to your axolotl to soak in, swim in, and drink.

in case you do not like the concept of buying bottled spring water, you do not have a opposite osmosis system in your kitchen sink, and don't have any filtration device like a refrigerator clear out, Brita, PUR, or Zero Water you have to both buy de-chlorination drops from the aquarium save, boil the water, or allow your water to take a seat for 12-24 hours earlier than putting it on your axolotl's enclosure. If you are nevertheless worried that there's chlorine within the water, you should purchase take a look at strips to check the level earlier to apply.

THE END

www.ingramcontent.com/pod-product-compliance
Lightning Source LLC
Chambersburg PA
CBHW070819170726
48000CB00018B/1403